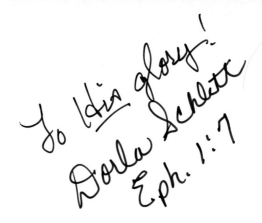

To His glory!
Dorla Schlitt
Eph. 1:7

Publishing services provided by Fitting Words, LLC
www.fittingwords.net

ISBN: 978-1-5710240-8-4

ACKNOWLEDGEMENTS

I want to thank and acknowledge my indebtedness to Richard Booker. For it is in reading his book, *The Miracle of the Scarlet Thread*, that I was inspired to write and share with children and youth the profound love and sovereignty of God in bringing salvation to mankind through Jesus Christ.

I also want to thank the Children's Ministry staffs and pastoral ministers I came to love and serve with for almost 40 years. Over those years I grew in deeper understanding of the relationship between the Old and New Testament being one story and I am forever grateful.

My heart overflows with thankfulness for my family who encouraged me in ministry to children and participated in many VBS programs as both young participants and as volunteers!

John, I love you! You are my sweet encourager in every endeavor I undertake!

Most significant is my Jesus! You gave me life and fill my heart with joy! There is nothing greater than knowing and loving you!

Booker, Richard. *The Miracle of the Scarlet Thread.* Destiny Image Publishers, 1981.

COME ALONG WITH ME
AS WE LOOK FOR A "SCARLET THREAD"
THAT WEAVES THROUGH THE BIBLE FROM
BEGINNING TO END.
FROM THE GARDEN OF EDEN
AND THE PROMISE GOD MADE,
WE FOLLOW THE SCRIPTURES
TO SHOW US THE WAY.
THE GOD OF THE BIBLE
IS LOVING AND GOOD.
IN HIS TIME AND
BY HIS HAND,
GOD SENT JESUS
TO RESCUE MAN.
SO, COME ALONG WITH ME
AND LET'S FIND THE CLUES
OF HOW THE OLD TESTAMENT STORIES POINT
US TO NEW TESTAMENT TRUTH.
IT IS THERE THAT WE LEARN
THE FULFILLMENT OF GOD'S PLAN
TO RESCUE US FROM DEATH
AND BRING US HOME TO HIM AGAIN.

THE GARDEN OF EDEN: ADAM & EVE

"The Lord is trustworthy in all he promises
and faithful in all he does."

PSALM 145:13

IN THE BEGINNING GOD created the earth to be a beautiful world. Upon a portion of the earth God planted a garden in the east called Eden. Within the Garden of Eden God created animals of all kinds and many beautiful plants and trees that were pleasing to the eye and produced food to eat.

The garden was also the home of God's most precious creation called man. God created man, male and female. God called man Adam and Eve. God created them even more special than all creation. God gave them a body to enjoy His world and breathed life into them.

He gave them a spirit to have a relationship with Him and a soul to think, feel, and make choices.

Under God's authority man was given the honor to steward or care for all the earth. God loved Adam and Eve very much and provided for all their needs. In the center of the garden were two beautiful trees. The tree of life produced fruit giving life when eaten. The tree of the knowledge of good and evil produced beautiful fruit that was much different.

God told Adam and Eve they could eat from any of the trees in the garden except from the tree of knowledge of good and evil. If Adam and Eve chose to disobey God and eat from that tree, God said they would surely die. God's word to Adam and Eve was clear. THE PAYMENT FOR SIN IS DEATH.

Even though Adam and Eve did not know what "death" meant, they did know God was good and He loved them very much. God's Word was to warn and protect them. Adam and Eve were happy in the garden and enjoyed their special relationship with God.

One day Satan came to Eve. Satan, a spirit being, had made himself look like one of the serpents in the garden. Satan hated God. Satan wanted to rule over all the earth. He wanted the authority and honor God had given to man. Satan devised a plan.

Satan tempted Eve to sin by disobeying God. Satan lied to Eve and said she would not die from eating the fruit of the forbidden tree. Eve wanted very much to taste that beautiful fruit so she chose to believe the lie and doubt the truth of God's Word. Eve ate from the tree of good and evil. When Eve offered the fruit to Adam, he also made the choice to disobey God's Word. Adam ate the fruit too. When they disobeyed God's good and protective Word, everything changed for them.

As soon as they ate the fruit that was forbidden, Adam and Eve realized they had sinned by disobeying God's Word to them and deserved death. They made coverings of fig leaves and tried to hide from God. God is not like man. God is a spirit, invisible to our eyes and present everywhere. Nothing is hidden from Him. God knew what Adam and Eve had done and He knew they were hiding from Him.

God did not strike them dead out of anger for disobeying Him. Instead, God sought them and called them out from hiding into the light. When they came, neither one admitted their own sin nor asked God's forgiveness. Each made excuses for what they had done.

GOD KNEW THE TRUTH.

The leaf coverings Adam and Eve had made with their own hands were not acceptable to God. Adam and Eve could not change what had taken place. Their sin deserved death and they knew it. What happened? The Bible tells us that even though God is loving and full of mercy toward man, He is also just in all His ways. The word "justice" means to make something right again requiring a penalty.

7.

8.

Out of love and mercy God provided an innocent and pure animal from the garden to shed its blood as a substitute for Adam and Eve's death temporarily satisfying the penalty of death for their sin. The Bible tells us the LIFE OF ALL CREATURES IS IN THE BLOOD. WITHOUT THE SHEDDING OF BLOOD SIN CANNOT BE FORGIVEN. (HEBREWS 9:22)

God then covered Adam and Eve with the animal's skin. Although Adam and Eve were spared from immediate death, sin had entered their soul and spirit, often called the heart of man. From that time forward everything changed.

The Bible tells us all mankind and the earth itself would experience the results of sin. Man's physical body would grow old, wear out, and die. The body and soul would experience pain, suffering, sickness, and disease. Thorns and poisonous plants, deadly plagues, volcanoes, and earthquakes are all part of the curse upon the earth. The Bible tells us the earth "groans" to be set free from death and decay.

Most sadly of all, the spirit of man became dead to God. No longer could man enjoy the special relationship he once had with God. Sin now separated man from God. Because sin had entered the heart of man, man's desire was no longer to honor God out of love for Him. Now, man wanted to honor himself by choosing his own way.

God told Adam and Eve they would have to leave the Garden of Eden. God placed a cherubim angel with a flaming sword to guard the entrance of the Garden. God wanted to protect Adam and Eve from returning to the garden, eating from the tree of life, and living forever separated from him.

That's not all God told Adam, Eve, and Satan. Before Adam and Eve left the Garden, God gave a very important and glorious promise. IN GENESIS 3:15 GOD PROMISED TO SOMEDAY SEND A SAVIOR WHO WOULD SHED HIS OWN BLOOD AS A SUBSTITUTE FOR MAN AND PROVIDE COMPLETE FORGIVENESS OF SIN.

This Savior would defeat or "crush" Satan, sin, and death forever. Through the Savior the way would be made available for the relationship between God and all mankind to be restored back again permanently! God's plan was ultimately good for man. How do we know? Let's find out!

EGYPT & THE PASSOVER

"For the wages of sin is death."

ROMANS 6:23

Time has passed since Adam and Eve lived. Many generations of families have filled the earth. Through those years many people worshipped God but many did not. Many chose to worship other things, not the one true living God. There was a man named Abraham who lived in the land of Ur. Abraham was not a perfect man but he obeyed and worshipped the one true living God.

One night GOD SPOKE TO ABRAHAM AND SAID, "LOOK UP AT THE HEAVENS AND COUNT THE STARS... SO SHALL YOUR DESCENDANTS BE." (GENESIS 15:15) God chose to make a special agreement with Abraham called a covenant. God promised to be faithful to His covenant with Abraham and Abraham believed God. God promised to have a people for Himself through Abraham's descendants. God did just that!

12.

GOD'S PEOPLE WERE CALLED ISRAELITES.

Over a thousand years later in the land called Egypt there was an evil Pharaoh who ruled over the Israelites. This evil Pharaoh did not worship the one true God whom the Israelites worshipped. He worshipped many different kinds of false gods.

The Israelite people had grown in great numbers and were forced to work very hard for the Pharaoh as slaves. As time passed the evil Pharaoh became so afraid of being overtaken by the great numbers of Israelite slaves, he ordered all the Israelite baby boys killed. One Israelite mother, trusting the one true God to protect and spare her baby boy's life, made a woven basket coated with tar and pitch so that it would float on the river Nile. She placed her baby boy in it and hid the basket in the reeds. Do you know this baby boy's name?

God protected and provided for Moses. Moses' sister, Miriam, hid in the bulrushes and watched over Moses from the bank of the river. When Moses was found floating in the river by Pharaoh's daughter, Miriam went to her and asked if she needed a woman to care for Moses.

Pharaoh's daughter said "Yes!" Miriam rushed to bring her mother. God provided a way for Moses' true mother and family to care for him and teach him about the one true God. When Moses was old enough, he went to live in Pharaoh's household with the Pharaoh's daughter who raised him as her son.

Moses grew to be a man and saw the suffering of his people as slaves. One day he watched as an Egyptian beat an Israelite slave. Moses was so angry he killed the Egyptian and hid his body in the sand. The next day when an Israelite told Moses what he had seen him do, Moses ran in fear to the desert where he cared for and watched over sheep for 40 years!

Did you know sheep are much like people? Sheep are stubborn, willful, and want their own way. A good shepherd must learn to be patient, understanding of a sheep's nature, and willing to lead his sheep with kindness and authority.

During those years God was preparing Moses for his future. The Israelite people had been praying for over 400 years asking God to deliver or rescue them from slavery. God heard the groanings and prayers of His people all those years. WHEN THE TIME WAS RIGHT, GOD ANSWERED THEIR PRAYERS.

One day while Moses was still in the desert and tending his sheep, he saw flames coming from a bush a short distance away. Why would this be strange? The bush kept burning and burning! Moses went over to investigate. As he drew near the burning bush, he heard his name being called, "Moses, Moses!"

"Here I am!" he answered, not knowing who was calling him. God spoke to Moses out of the burning bush and said, "Don't come any closer. Take off your sandals for you are standing on holy ground. I am the God of your ancestors, Abraham, Isaac, and Jacob." (Exodus 3:5) God told Moses, "I am sending you to Pharaoh. I WILL DELIVER MY PEOPLE out of Egypt and slavery. I will lead them into a good land and they will worship Me."

"Who am I to go before Pharaoh? And, when I go to the children of Israel, they will ask who sent me? What is his name? What shall I say?"

God replied, "I AM THAT I AM." I AM hath sent me to you. The Lord God of your fathers, the God of Abraham, the God of Isaac, and the God of Jacob hath sent me." Moses responded, "Please, Lord, I am not a good speaker. I speak slowly and my tongue makes it difficult for me to speak." "No, it is you," God answered Moses.

God would help Moses to do His will and fulfill the purpose God had for him. Moses must learn to trust God to help him in his weakness. Who is being sent to lead God's people out of Egypt? How do you think this will be accomplished? By Moses' strong words? By God's power? Moses obeyed God and returned to Egypt.

God provided Aaron, Moses' brother, to help him speak before Pharaoh ten separate times. Each time Pharaoh denied the Israelites freedom, God sent a plague.

The first plague turned the Nile River to blood. As a result, fish died and the people could not drink from it. Plagues of frogs, lice, flies, pestilence, boils, hail, locusts, and darkness were also sent by God.

With each plague God showed His power over the many false gods the Egyptians worshipped. After the 9th plague Moses told Pharaoh the worst plague of all would come upon Egypt if he did not relent and allow the Israelites to leave. Pharaoh still said, "No!" As a result of Pharaoh again denying the Israelites permission to leave Egypt, God told Moses what was going to happen. At midnight the firstborn sons of Egypt would die, including Pharaoh's son. GOD WOULD SAVE HIS PEOPLE FROM DEATH through a miracle called THE PASSOVER.

What is the "PASSOVER"? Let's find out!

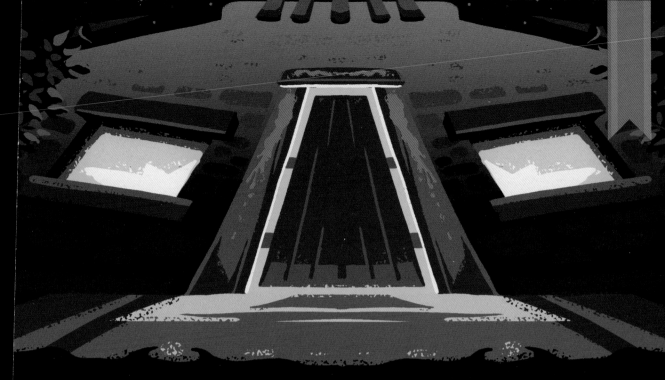

God gave the Israelites these instructions. Each Israelite family was to choose A SPOTLESS AND PURE MALE LAMB and sacrifice it. The lamb's blood was to be smeared on the doorposts and lintel of their homes. Inside each home they were to share a special Passover meal together. There were thousands of Israelite families who would follow God's instructions that night.

At midnight God sent the Angel of Death through the land to strike down the firstborn Egyptians. The angel would see the blood of the lamb covering the top and sides of the doorway of the Israelite homes and "pass over" them. God would not allow death to enter. Even though the people inside the home might have been afraid, deliverance or rescue from death is based on obedience and faith in God's Word... not on their emotions or feelings.

The Passover made a distinction between the Egyptians and God's people. God provided a way for His people to be delivered or rescued from death. After the Passover took place, Pharaoh ordered all of the Israelites to leave Egypt! They were free! They took their belongings, their flocks and herds, the gifts of gold, and the provisions the Egyptian people gave them. There were about 600,000 Israelite men along with women, children, and a mixed multitude of others who quickly left Egypt.

God commanded His people to celebrate "The Passover" each year with a special meal called a Seder. It was a special feast to remember how God had delivered them from death.

THE WILDERNESS
& THE TABERNACLE

"For the life of the creature is in the blood, and I have given it to you to make atonement for yourselves on the altar; It is the blood that makes atonement for one's life."

LEVITICUS 17:11

God's almighty power miraculously saved all the Israelite people from death and brought them out of Egypt. Thousands of Israelites began the journey to the land God promised Abraham long ago. The Israelite people were happy and excited to leave Egypt. Their prayers had been answered.

As the Israelites traveled away from Egypt, God went ahead of them. His presence with them was symbolized in a column of fire to give them light for both day and night. The fire produced a cloud of smoke in the day to follow and a column of fire at night to keep them warm in the desert and light their way.

Just as the Israelite people had gotten started on their journey, Pharaoh changed his mind and sent his soldiers after them. Pharaoh wanted the Israelites to come back and serve him again. The Israelite people could see the Red Sea in front of them and the Egyptian soldiers closing in behind them. They were afraid and wanted to return to Egypt.

Moses answered them, "Don't be afraid. Stand firm and you will see the deliverance the Lord will bring you today. The Egypt you see today you will never see again. The Lord will fight for you, you need only to be still." (Exodus 14:13-14) God told Moses to raise his staff and stretch out his arm over the sea. God divided the water to the left and to the right. All the Israelites passed through safely to dry ground.

As Egyptian soldiers entered the Red Sea, God brought the water down upon all of the soldiers and they were no more. The Israelite people sang songs of thanksgiving and praise to God for His mighty power. The women danced with joy for the victory won by God. Moses and the Israelites continued their journey to the land God promised Abraham and all his descendants. Even though there were shorter routes through the desert wilderness, God chose to lead them to their destination by way of a longer route. GOD KNEW WHAT WAS BEST FOR HIS PEOPLE.

God was good to His people. He provided water from a rock. Daily bread called "manna" fell from heaven. Quail was their meat.

When they came to a mountain called Mt. Sinai, the mountain shook and was covered with smoke. God had come down upon it in fire and the people were afraid. God called Moses up the mountain. On the mountain God gave Moses the laws for His people to obey called The TEN COM-MANDMENTS. The Ten Commandments were given so that people would recognize and know what sin is.

SIN IS DISOBEYING GOD'S WORD AND CHOOSING OUR OWN WAY. THE PEOPLE LEARNED THAT NO ONE COULD COMPLETELY KEEP GOD'S LAW. ALL PEOPLE SIN.

After God gave the Ten Commandments, He gave Moses' instructions to build a sanctuary called the tabernacle. The tabernacle would be a special place God's presence would dwell and sin sacrifices would be made.

God provided a way for the sins of all the people to be temporarily covered each year. God gave special directions to Moses in how the tabernacle was to be built and what was to be inside. All the people contributed their talents and their goods to build it. Although it was very plain and not attractive on the outside, the inside was beautiful. Each item inside the tabernacle pointed to the Promised Savior and had a special purpose.

Inside the tabernacle was a special place called the Holiest of Holies. The Holiest of Holies was separated from the rest of the tabernacle by a veil or curtain. Within the Holiest of Holies was the Ark of the Covenant where God's presence dwelled. Once a year the High Priest who served in the tabernacle made a sin offering to God for himself and for the people's sin. The ceremony required two spotless goats. The High Priest would cast lots to determine which goat would die and which one would be released.

The High Priest would take the blood of the sacrificed goat behind the veil into the Holiest of Holies. He would sprinkle the blood on the mercy seat of the Ark. As long as the people heard the bells jingle on the hem of his garment, they knew he was alive, the sin offering was being made, and their sins would be covered or atoned for another year.

The second goat called the "scapegoat" did not die. According to Jewish history a red strip of cloth was tied to the scapegoat. The red strip represented the red blood that was sprinkled on the mercy seat. The High Priest would lay his hand on the goat symbolically transferring the sins of the people to the animal. The goat was released into the wilderness symbolically carrying away the people's sins... never to be seen again.

This was a visible sign to the people that their sins were atoned for or covered and separated from them for another year. This day was called the Day of Atonement.

The tabernacle was also portable. Everything in the tabernacle could be packed up and moved with the Israelites as they traveled. When they stopped for a period of time it would be set up again with all the Israelite family tents around it. God's presence would always go with His people.

JERICHO & THE STORY OF RAHAB

"For he has rescued us from the dominion of darkness and brought us into the kingdom of the Son he loves, in whom we have forgiveness of sin."

COLOSSIANS 1:13-14

Through the desert wilderness God led Moses and the Israelites. As the Israelites approached the land God had promised Abraham long ago, God told Moses to send twelve spies to explore this land called Canaan. The men were gone for forty days. When the spies returned, they reported the land to have an abundance of fruit and food. They also reported the people lived in walled cities and were not only strong but of great size. All the spies, except for two named Joshua and Caleb, were afraid to enter the new land and lied calling the people "giants."

Joshua and Caleb were not like the other men. They were confident and sure that God would be with them, lead them into the land, and help them overtake the enemies who lived there.

The Israelites grumbled and complained. They didn't believe what Joshua and Caleb said and they wanted to stone them. GOD WAS NOT PLEASED that His people did not trust Him. Only Caleb and Joshua trusted God.

As a result, God told Moses that neither he nor the Israelite people would be able to enter the promised land of Canaan. The Israelites would remain as shepherds wandering in the wilderness desert for forty years—one year for each of the forty days.

Within the next forty years Moses and the generation of people who had not trusted God died. At that time God appointed Joshua to lead His people into the promised land and conquer the enemies living there. The first enemy to conquer was the city of Jericho.

Jericho was a city surrounded by a great wall. Joshua sent two spies ahead to ford the Jordan River and enter the walled city. The spies entered the city and came to the house of Rahab, a sinful woman.

When soldiers came looking for the spies, Rahab hid them on her roof under stalks of flax and directed the soldiers away from her house. Afterwards Rahab told the spies, "I know the Lord has given this land to you and that a great fear of you has fallen on us. For the Lord, your God, is God of heaven above and on the earth below." (Joshua 2:9, 11)

RAHAB BELIEVED GOD was who He said He was. She asked the spies for a way that she and her family could be delivered or saved from death. The spies told Rahab to bind a scarlet or red cord from her balcony window. If she obeyed, she and her family inside the house would be saved from death when the Israelites took the city. The spies slipped out of the city safely. They crossed back over the Jordan river and returned to Joshua with their report.

Joshua readied the Israelites to set out for Jericho. As they came to the Jordan River God gave instructions to Joshua. God would part the waters for them as He had done at the Red Sea. This time, the priests carrying the Ark of the Covenant would step first into the water's edge. The Jordan River would part on both sides and all the soldiers and people would walk safely to the riverbank. The people would surely know that GOD'S PRESENCE WAS WITH THEM.

When all had passed through, one man from each of the 12 tribes of Israel was instructed to go back to the riverbed where the priests stood with the Ark. Each man brought out from the riverbed a large stone to make a marker memorial to what the Lord had done for His people. After this the priests carried the Ark onto the riverbank and the river resumed flowing.

As Joshua approached the edge of Jericho, he saw what seemed to be a man with a sword. Joshua said to him, "Are you for us or for our enemies?" The man identified himself as Commander of the army of the Lord. He was not under the authority of man but under the authority of God and had been sent with a message for Joshua. He commanded Joshua to remove his sandals as the place he stood was holy. Then the Lord spoke to Joshua saying, "I have delivered Jericho into your hands along with its king and fighting men." (Joshua 6:2)

God gave Joshua instructions in how to go and take the walled city. THE VICTORY BELONGED TO GOD AND HIM ALONE. JOSHUA AND THE PEOPLE WERE ONLY TO OBEY.

For six days armed Israelite soldiers went ahead and behind seven priests blowing their ram horn trumpets and the priests carrying the Ark. Each day they marched around the city wall without saying one word. The only sound were the trumpets announcing God's presence. On the seventh day after marching silently around the city seven times with the trumpets sounding, Joshua gave the final order. With the long trumpet blast Joshua told the people "Shout, for God has given you the city!" (Joshua 6:16)

Everyone obeyed and the walls came tumbling down!
When the walls of Jericho fell, Joshua sent the two spies to Rahab's house. The spies saw the scarlet or red cord, and rescued Rahab and her family. Because of Rahab's faith in Israel's God and her obedience in hanging the scarlet cord from her window, she and her family escaped death. Rahab was adopted into God's family of Israelites and later married an Israelite man. Rahab is part of the family line of Jesus!

THE COMING OF
THE PROMISED SAVIOR

"The Lord has done what he planned;
he has fulfilled his word, which he decreed
long ago..."

LAMENTATIONS 2:17A

More than a thousand years have passed. Kings and kingdoms of men rise and fall. Men of God document Israel's ancient history of God dealing with His people and His enemies. God's plan for His creation and the Promised Savior's arrival is moving forward. All through Old Testament history don't you imagine God's people must have been wondering... When will He come? Where will we see Him? What will He be like? What will He do? How will things change?

In the book of Jeremiah of the Old Testament, God speaks through His prophet saying a new covenant will come with the arrival and work of the Promised Savior. Jeremiah prophesied that the Old Testament covenant of laws written on stone and the temporary sin offerings would pass away. God's new covenant would be made in the hearts of people. God would give them faith to believe and trust in the Promised Savior for forgiveness of sin.

With the closure of the Old Testament of the Bible, something new and wonderful was about to happen!

"...WHEN THE TIME HAD FULLY COME, GOD SENT HIS SON, BORN OF A WOMAN, BORN UNDER THE LAW TO REDEEM THOSE UNDER THE LAW..." GALATIANS 4:4,5A

In the still and quiet of an ordinary night, God's Word to the prophets was fulfilled. The Son of God, miraculously conceived by the Holy Spirit in the womb of a virgin named Mary, had come to pass. He who is the visible image of the invisible God, came from heaven and was born in the flesh, a baby. Mary, His mother, and Joseph, her husband, gave Him the name Jesus, Emmanuel.... God with us. The Promised Savior had arrived!

On that night His birth was known to only a few. Shepherds in a nearby field watching over their sheep witnessed a burst of glorious light in the sky above them. Though frightened they gladly received an angel's message to them of the Savior's birth in Bethlehem, the city of David. As a whole host of angels appeared singing and praising God, the shepherds' hearts were assured and they hurriedly left to find and worship this newborn king.

Magi in the east who studied the stars saw an unusually bright star in the night sky and began a journey to follow it. After some time, they came to Jerusalem and asked King Herod where they might find this newborn King of the Jews the prophets had spoken about. King Herod being afraid of a threat to his kingship inquired of the High Priest and teachers of the law. They told him "Bethlehem."   King Herod sent the Magi there and told them to return to him.

Continuing on to follow the star their long journey brought them to a house in Bethlehem where they found Jesus, the child, and His mother. In presenting Jesus with gifts of gold, frankincense, and myrrh they worshipped Him. Having had a dream warning them not to return to King Herod with their news, the Magi left for their homeland by a different way.

Soon after the Magi's visit, an angel warned Joseph to leave Bethlehem with Mary and Jesus. To escape King Herod's evil plan to kill Jesus they traveled to Egypt. After King Herod's death an angel instructed Joseph to take his family back to Israel to the town of Nazareth in the district of Galilee.

A third one who knew of the Promised Savior's arrival was Satan himself. In the Garden of Eden God had promised Satan's eventual defeat by the coming Promised Savior. Satan, a deceiving and lying spirit, had devised and implemented various schemes throughout the ages to prevent God's plan for the salvation of man to be completed. Satan's efforts were to no avail. The scriptures tell us that our loving and faithful God does not lie.

"BUT THE PLANS OF THE LORD STAND FIRM FOREVER, THE PURPOSES OF HIS HEART THROUGH ALL GENERATIONS." PSALM. 33:11

Jesus, God's Son, was raised by Mary and Joseph in Nazareth. At the age of thirty Jesus stepped away from the carpentry shop where He had been trained as a skilled carpenter by Joseph, His earthly father. He left His home in Nazareth. Jesus' life path now led in a different direction.

Jesus went to the Jordan River where John the Baptist was preaching and telling people to repent or turn from their sins for the kingdom of heaven is near. UPON SEEING JESUS, JOHN CALLED OUT, "LOOK, THE LAMB OF GOD WHO TAKES AWAY THE SIN OF THE WORLD…" (JOHN 1:29) John then baptized Jesus in the Jordan River and as he did, the Holy Spirit descended on Jesus in the form of a dove.

A voice from heaven spoke. "This is my Son, whom I love; with Him I am well pleased." (Matthew 3:17)

Just after His baptism, Jesus was led by the Holy Spirit from the Jordan River to the desert. During the next forty days and nights Jesus was alone and ate nothing. While there Satan came to Jesus and tempted Him three times to sin by disobeying God's Word. Unlike Adam who dis-obeyed God's Word and sinned when tempted, Jesus chose to obey God's

In the next three years, Jesus called twelve ordinary men to follow Him as disciples. As they traveled from town to town they were always with Jesus. Along with the crowds of people, the disciples heard Jesus teach about God and His kingdom. They witnessed the many miracles of healing Jesus did for the broken and hurting people. They saw the love, compassion, and power of Jesus.

Even though the disciples did not understand all of the deep truth and parables Jesus spoke about with them, they knew Jesus was their friend and trusted Him to be who he said he was. He was more than a teacher. HE IS THE SON OF GOD.

Often times Jesus would spend time away from the crowds alone with His Heavenly Father in prayer. Jesus knew where His life was heading and He drew strength from this special time. As the last week of Jesus' earthly life approached, He shared with His disciples that they were going to Jerusalem for the Passover and while there He would suffer many things... even death. Yet, He would be raised to life! They could not understand how this could be.

With Jesus' humble entry into Jerusalem on a lowly donkey, the week held many events. Jesus continued speaking God's Word to the crowds and to individuals as He went about doing God's will in spite of those who opposed Him. All the while Satan was working his evil in the hearts of men to trap and kill Jesus.

At the end of the week during the traditional yearly Passover meal Jesus shared many things with His disciples. Jesus spoke of leaving them, but told them not to fear. Jesus promised them He would send the Holy Spirit to comfort, teach, enable, and guide them and all those who trusted in His name. At the end of the meal, Jesus took a towel and washed the feet of the disciples. As He did so, He told them that in order for them to be part of Him, He must wash them. Again, the disciples did not understand.

Before the end of the evening, Jesus knew and spoke of one who would betray Him. Judas, one of His own disciples, yielded to Satan's temptation to sin and betray Jesus.

After the Passover meal Jesus took a few disciples with Him and walked to the Garden of Gethsemane. Leaving the disciples to sit and keep watch, Jesus walked on to a place He could pray.

In the Garden of Gethsemane even as Jesus prayed in anguish knowing what was to come, He chose to obey God, His Father, saying, "May your will be done." (Luke 22:42) What began in the Garden of Eden with Adam's disobedience ended in the Garden of Gethsemane with Jesus willingly choosing to obey God's will. "FOR I HAVE COME DOWN FROM HEAVEN NOT TO DO MY WILL BUT TO DO THE WILL OF HIM WHO SENT ME." JOHN. 6:38

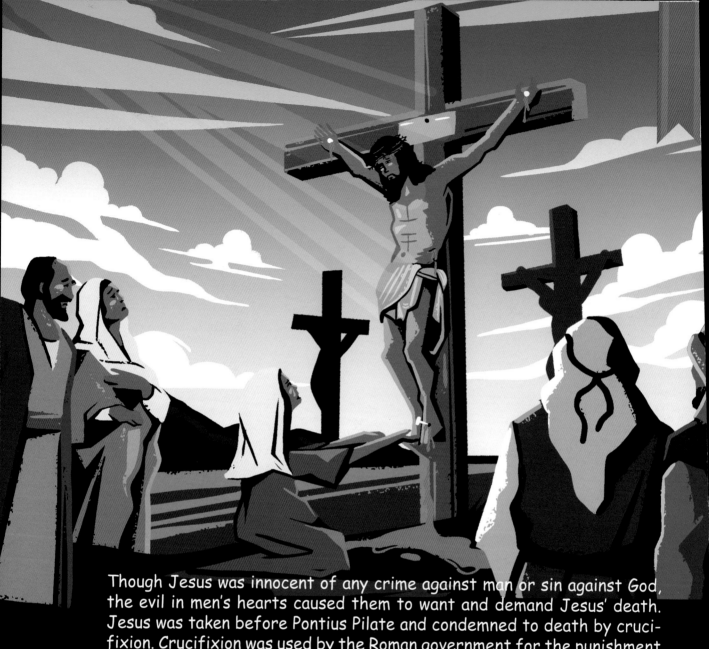

Though Jesus was innocent of any crime against man or sin against God, the evil in men's hearts caused them to want and demand Jesus' death. Jesus was taken before Pontius Pilate and condemned to death by crucifixion. Crucifixion was used by the Roman government for the punishment of criminals. It was a very painful and long-suffering death.

Jesus was beaten, spit upon, and a crown of thorns mocking His kingship was placed on His head. Jesus carried his own cross until He was unable to do so. A man standing nearby named Simon of Cyrene was forced by Roman soldiers to help him.

At Golgotha, the Place of the Skull, Jesus hung on the cross. Satan used the words of a Roman soldier to tempt Him one last time. "If you are the King of the Jews, save yourself," (Luke 23:37) he said. Jesus remained nailed to the cross. His last words being...

"IT IS FINISHED." JOHN 19:30

With Jesus' death, Satan thought he had finally destroyed this One who had come to set men free of sin and death! But that is not so! Taken to a borrowed tomb after His death on the cross, Jesus' body lay until the third day. On the third day, just as He had told the disciples earlier, God raised Him from the dead!

Jesus, raised in the flesh, appeared to many and spoke to His disciples before ascending into heaven to sit at the right hand of God the Father Almighty! Jesus, the Promised Savior, spoken of in Genesis 3:15, had come and completed what God had sent Him, His one and only Son, to do on earth.

Jesus, sinless and pure, referred to as the "Lamb of God" by John the Baptist, willingly bore the wrath of God for sin. In doing so Jesus paid the penalty of the law, making forgiveness of sin and a restored relationship with God possible. With the resurrection of Jesus from death, death was defeated! Jesus made forgiveness of sin and eternal life available to all who trust Him as their own Savior.

"FOR MY FATHER'S WILL IS THAT EVERYONE WHO LOOKS TO THE SON AND BELIEVES IN HIM SHALL HAVE ETERNAL LIFE...." JOHN 6:40

The Adventure of the Scarlet Thread began in the Garden of Eden with God's promise in Genesis 3:15 to send a Savior who would crush or defeat Satan's power over sin and death. The Scarlet Thread runs through the Old Testament scriptures where the covenant law required a yearly animal blood sacrifice to temporarily cover man's sin. These sacrifices pointed forward in time to the shed blood of the Promised Savior, Jesus Christ. Do you see the Scarlet Thread weaving through the scriptures of the four Old Testament stories?

The Scarlet Thread is a symbol of the provision God made for sin until the Savior's arrival. The Adventure of the Scarlet Thread culminates in the New Testament with the birth, death, resurrection, and ascension of Jesus Christ.

With the shedding of Jesus' blood for the forgiveness of sin, the law with the penalty of death for sin was cancelled forever and the old covenant was replaced with a new covenant based on faith in Jesus Christ, the Savior of the world. All those who by faith believe Jesus Christ died for their sin become sons and daughters in the covenant family of God and will dwell with Him forever. They will never be separated from God again!

"AFTER THIS I LOOKED, AND THERE BEFORE ME WAS A GREAT MULTITUDE THAT NO ONE COULD COUNT, FROM EVERY NATION, TRIBE, PEOPLE AND LANGUAGE, STANDING BEFORE THE THRONE AND BEFORE THE LAMB. THEY WERE WEARING WHITE ROBES AND WERE HOLDING PALM BRANCHES IN THEIR HANDS."
REVELATION 7:9

THE ADVENTURE OF THE SCARLETT THREAD

The Adventure of the Scarlet Thread: Educator's Guide is an accompaniment to The *Adventure of the Scarlet Thread: The Promise Fulfilled.*

This guide is helpful to those who wish to expand the learning experience. Adult leader resources provide guidance in introducing and reviewing each story enabling greater depth of learning for student participation. Opportunities for activities, crafts, and games enrich the experience of learning about God's great love, faithfulness, and provision for them through His Son, Jesus Christ.